The Ladybird G
Presid
the United States
E PLURIBUS
UNUM
Ladybird
D0613011
MCPL-HM
3 2611 050632898

TABLE OF CONTENTS

George Washington became the first president of the United States of America in 1789. Since then, the American people have elected a president every four years. The framers of the **Constitution** made America a **democracy**, with a government of officials—including the president—chosen by the people.

The president (chief executive) heads the executive branch of the government. **Congress**, made up of the **Senate** and the **House of Representatives**, is the legislative, or law-making, branch. The **Supreme Court** is the judicial branch. The power of each branch of government is limited—or checked—by a system of **checks and balances**.

The president's four-year term limits the power of the executive branch. The chief executive may serve two four-year terms. He can **veto** a **bill** passed by Congress, checking the power of the legislature. But Congress can override a presidential veto, with a two-thirds majority vote. The Supreme Court provides balance by judging whether laws and **amendments** are constitutional.

The president of the U.S. has the most important and most difficult job in the country. The president works with Congress to make laws that govern the economy. The president defines and shapes foreign policy. With the approval of the Senate, the president makes treaties with other nations and appoints ambassadors and Supreme Court judges. As the commander in chief of the armed forces, the president can send troops to foreign countries, but it is Congress that has the power to declare war.

The presidency is a demanding, challenging, and exciting job.

You Can Be President If:

- ★ You are a natural-born citizen of the U.S.A.
- ★ You have lived in the U.S. for at least 14 years.
- ★ You are at least 35 years old.

VITAL STATS

Birthday: February 22, 1732
State: Virginia
Political party: Federalist
Vice president: John Adams
Age at inauguration: 57

Wife: Martha Dandridge Custis
Children: Jacky and Patsy (stepchildren)
Date and cause of death:
December 14, 1799; pneumonia

HISTORICAL HAPPENINGS

★ 1789: Washington took office in New York City, the first capital of the U.S.

★ 1791: The Bill of Rights was added to the Constitution. Its purpose was to protect the rights of individuals from governmental interference.

Revolutionary War Hero: As commander in chief, George Washington led the colonial armies against the British in the American War of Independence. After several important victories, Washington and his men—who served without pay—spent a harsh winter in Valley Forge, eating soup made of burned leaves and dirt. Then Washington joined forces with the French troops of Comte de Rochambeau, and after four years of fighting, forced British General Charles Cornwallis to surrender.

Yes, Your Presidentness . . .

When the first president was elected, no one knew how to address him. Here are a few of Congress's early suggestions: His Elective Majesty, His Elective Highness, His Highness the President of the United States and Protector of the Rights of the Same, and Your Mightiness. Today, it's Mr. President and Sir. The vote is still out on what the first woman president will be called.

FASCINATING FACTS

✪ George Washington never chopped down a cherry tree. Mason Weems invented that story in the early 1800s for his book, *Life of George Washington; with Curious Anecdotes, Equally Honorable to Himself and Exemplary to His Young Countrymen.*

✪ Washington had many pairs of false teeth, some of which were made of wood.

VITAL STATS

Birthday: October 30, 1735
State: Massachusetts
Political party: Federalist
Vice president: Thomas Jefferson
Age at inauguration: 61
Wife: Abigail Smith
Children: Abigail Amelia, John Quincy, Susanna, Charles, Thomas Boylston
Date and cause of death: July 4, 1826; natural causes

HISTORICAL HAPPENINGS

★ 1796: Adams was a member of the **Federalist party**, which favored giving the central government power over the individual states. He ran against Thomas Jefferson, winning by three electoral votes. In those days, the runner-up became vice president.

★ 1797: Adams helped establish the system of checks and balances that keeps the president, Congress, and the Supreme Court from having too much power.

A contest was held to find the best design for a residence for the president. Thomas Jefferson was among the many architects who submitted their ideas. The winner was James Hoban, an Irish-American architect. He received a $500 prize for his work, which called for painting the house white and inspired a new name: the White House.

FASCINATING FACTS

✪ The Adams family was the first to live in an official presidential residence. They moved into the Executive Mansion—later named the White House—when only six rooms were finished.

✪ John Adams and Thomas Jefferson died on exactly the same day, July 4, 1826, the fiftieth anniversary of the signing of the Declaration of Independence.

VITAL STATS

Birthday: April 13, 1743
State: Virginia
Political party: Democratic-Republican
Vice presidents: Aaron Burr and George Clinton
Age at inauguration: 57
Wife: Martha Wayles Skelton
Children: Martha Washington, Jane Randolph, Marie Polly, Lucy Elizabeth I, and Lucy Elizabeth II
Date and cause of death: July 4, 1826; natural causes

HISTORICAL HAPPENINGS

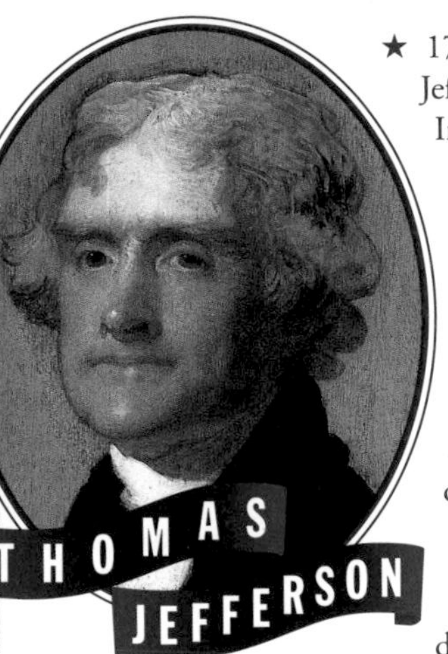

★ 1776: As a delegate to the Continental Congress, Jefferson wrote the first draft of the Declaration of Independence. It took him two weeks.

★ 1800: For the second time, Jefferson ran for president against his old friend and rival, John Adams. Jefferson ran as a member of the newly formed **Democratic-Republican party**. It favored limiting the power of the national government, greater autonomy for individuals and states, an alliance with France, and easy credit for debtors.

★ 1803: Jefferson negotiated the Louisiana Purchase with the French leader Napoleon, doubling the size of the United States. The price was 3¢ an acre.

FASCINATING FACTS

✪ Jefferson bathed his feet in cold water every morning to prevent colds. He ate more vegetables than meat, and drank a single glass of water every day.

✪ Jefferson is best known for his political leadership. But he was also an architect, farmer, inventor, fossil collector, diplomat, and scholar who could read several languages.

VITAL STATS

Birthday: March 15, 1751
State: Virginia
Political party: Democratic-Republican
Vice presidents: George Clinton and Elbridge Gerry
Age at inauguration: 57
Wife: Dorothea (Dolley) Payne Todd
Child: John Payne Todd (stepson)
Date and cause of death: June 28, 1836; natural causes

HISTORICAL HAPPENINGS

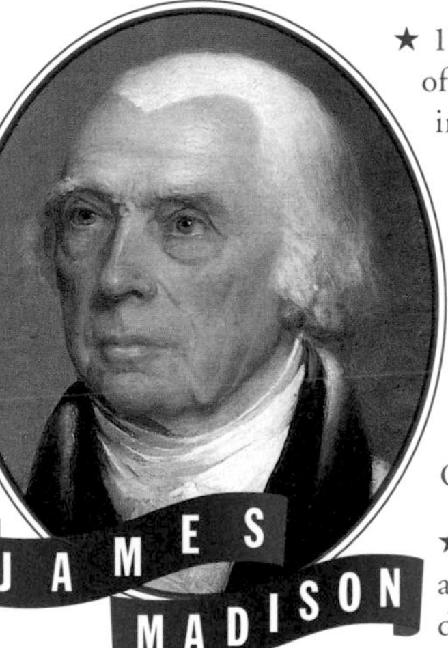

★ 1811: The U.S. turned against the British as a result of Britain's refusal to acknowledge America as an independent nation, British and French trade **embargoes**, prolonged conflict between Britain and France, and impressment—forced servitude of American men in the British navy. A faction in Congress began to argue for a declaration of war. This group became known as the War Hawks.

★ 1812: Provoked primarily by British interference in American shipping, tension with Great Britain erupted in the War of 1812.

★ 1814: British troops captured Washington, D.C., and set fire to the Executive Mansion. American defense of Fort McHenry inspired Francis Scott Key to write "The Star-Spangled Banner."

★ 1814: On Christmas Eve, the Treaty of Ghent was signed, ending the war. Because of poor communications, however, a British attack on New Orleans went on as planned. Two weeks later, U.S. retaliation, led by General Andrew Jackson, successfully—and finally—drove the British forces out.

FASCINATING FACT

✪ Both of Madison's vice presidents, George Clinton and Elbridge Gerry, died in office.

VITAL STATS

Birthday: April 28, 1758
State: Virginia
Political party: Democratic-Republican
Vice president: Daniel D. Tompkins
Age at inauguration: 58
Wife: Elizabeth Kortright
Children: Eliza, Maria Hester
Date and cause of death: July 4, 1831; natural causes

HISTORICAL HAPPENINGS

JAMES MONROE

★ 1821: The Missouri Compromise admitted Missouri to the U.S. as a slave state, but barred slavery in the rest of the territory acquired in the Louisiana Purchase.

★ 1823: Monroe's annual message to Congress outlined basic U.S. foreign policy. The Monroe Doctrine, as it is now known, proclaimed the Western Hemisphere off-limits to further colonization by European countries. It also made it absolutely clear that the U.S. was a legitimate country and a potential world power.

KEEP OUT!
KEEP OUT!

"The American continents, by the free and independent condition which they have assumed and maintain, are henceforth not to be considered as subjects for future colonization by any European powers." – Monroe Doctrine

FASCINATING FACTS

✪ James Monroe was the first president to tour the country. He traveled as far west as Detroit. He was also the first president to ride on a steamboat.

✪ Monroe was the third **Founding Father** to die on the Fourth of July.

VITAL STATS

Birthday: July 11, 1767
State: Massachusetts
Political party: Democratic-Republican
Vice president: John C. Calhoun
Age at inauguration: 57
Wife: Louisa Catherine Johnson
Children: George Washington, John Adams, Charles Francis, Louisa Catherine
Date and cause of death: February 23, 1848; stroke

HISTORICAL HAPPENINGS

JOHN QUINCY ADAMS

★ 1824: Five men, including Andrew Jackson, were on the ballot in this year's election. Not one candidate received a majority of electoral votes. Adams, supported by Speaker of the House Henry Clay, was selected by the House of Representatives. Adams named Clay his new Secretary of State, a move seen by some as evidence of a "corrupt bargain."

★ 1825-1829: Congress rejected all of the president's progressive ideas, including justice for slaves and Native Americans, a national system of roads and canals, a naval academy, and government aid for education.

★ 1825: The Democratic-Republican party, created by Thomas Jefferson to oppose the Federalists, split into two parties—the **Democratic party** and the **Whig party**.

Completed in 1825, the 360-mile-long Erie Canal connected New York harbor and the Hudson River with Lake Erie and the other Great Lakes, making it possible to ship goods from the East Coast to the Midwest.

FASCINATING FACTS

✪ When John Quincy Adams took the presidential oath on April 4, 1825, four of the five former presidents of the U.S. were still alive: John Adams (his father), Thomas Jefferson, James Madison, and James Monroe.

✪ John Quincy Adams was the only president whose father had also been president.

VITAL STATS

Birthday: March 15, 1767
State: South Carolina
Political party: Democratic
Vice presidents: John C. Calhoun and Martin Van Buren
Age at inauguration: 61
Wife: Rachel Donelson Robards
Children: None
Date and cause of death: June 8, 1845; natural causes

HISTORICAL HAPPENINGS

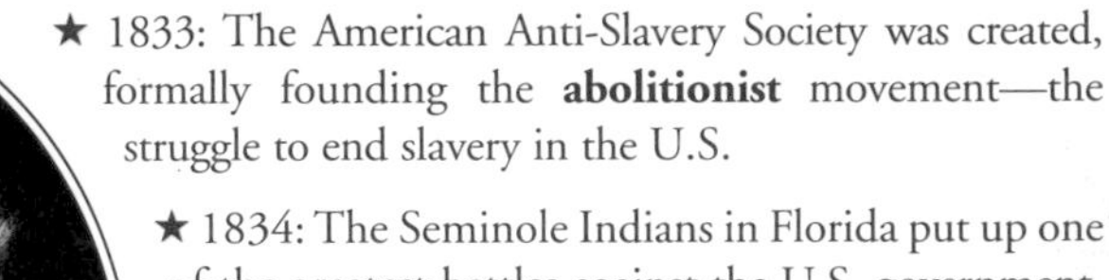

★ 1833: The American Anti-Slavery Society was created, formally founding the **abolitionist** movement—the struggle to end slavery in the U.S.

★ 1834: The Seminole Indians in Florida put up one of the greatest battles against the U.S. government. Though the U.S. eventually prevailed, there are still Seminoles in Florida today who claim they have never surrendered. Throughout his administrations, Jackson seized millions of acres of Native American land and broke countless treaties with the Indians.

★ 1836: The Alamo, a Spanish mission in San Antonio, was the site of the famous battle between Mexico and U.S. settlers for independence for Texas. All of the Texans, including Davy Crockett, were killed. Later that year, the Mexicans were defeated in the battle of San Jacinto, thereby establishing Texas as an independent republic.

FASCINATING FACTS

✪ Andrew Jackson's rough personality and leadership earned him the nickname Old Hickory.

✪ In 1835, Andrew Jackson survived the first attempt to **assassinate** a U.S. president.

✪ Jackson was the first president born in a log cabin.

VITAL STATS

Birthday: December 5, 1782
State: New York
Political party: Democratic
Vice president: Richard M. Johnson
Age at inauguration: 54
Wife: Hannah Hoes
Children: Abraham, John, Martin Jr., Smith Thompson
Date and cause of death: July 24, 1862; natural causes

HISTORICAL HAPPENINGS

MARTIN VAN BUREN

★ 1837: Financial panic swept the nation, caused by overspeculation in western land and canal and railroad construction. Banks failed, businesses closed, and unemployment increased. The depression that followed lasted until 1843.

★ 1840: Van Buren's opposition to federal aid to help businesses and his stand against annexing the Independent Republic of Texas led to the failure of his bid for reelection.

The Underground Railroad was neither underground nor a railroad. It was a secret system of routes set up to help slaves escape to freedom. Traveling on foot and usually at night, runaway slaves fled north, receiving food and shelter from homes established as "stations." Between 50,000 and 100,000 slaves "rode" the Underground Railroad.

UNDERGROUND RAILWAY– 1838

FASCINATING FACT

✪ Van Buren was known as the Little Magician and the Red Fox of Kinderhook because of his political skills.

9TH PRESIDENT OF THE UNITED STATES • TERM: 1841–DIED IN OFFICE

VITAL STATS

Birthday: February 9, 1773
State: Virginia
Political party: Whig
Vice president: John Tyler
Age at inauguration: 68
Wife: Anna Tuthill Symmes
Children: Elizabeth Bassett, John Cleves Symmes, Lucy Singleton, William H. Harrison Jr., John Scott, Benjamin, Mary Symmes, Carter Bassett, Anna Tuthill, James Findley
Date and cause of death: April 4, 1841; pneumonia

HISTORICAL HAPPENINGS

★ William Henry Harrison was the first president to die in office. He served only one month, the shortest term of any U.S. president.

FASCINATING FACTS: Harrison's nickname, Tippecanoe, came from the name of a battle he fought against the Shawnee Indians. "Tippecanoe and Tyler, too," his campaign slogan, remains one of the best known of American politics.

WILLIAM H. HARRISON

10TH PRESIDENT OF THE UNITED STATES • TERM: 1841–1845

VITAL STATS

Birthday: March 29, 1790
State: Virginia
Political party: Whig
Vice president: None
Age at inauguration: 51
Wives: Letitia Christian, Julia Gardiner
Children: With Letitia: Mary, Robert, John Jr., Letitia, Elizabeth, Anne Contesse, Alice, Tazewell. With Julia: David Gardiner, John Alexander, Julia, Lachlan, Lyon Gardiner, Robert Fitzwalter, Pearl
Date and cause of death: January 18, 1862; bronchitis

HISTORICAL HAPPENINGS

★1842: The Webster-Ashburton Treaty between the U.S. and Great Britain settled the line of the northeast border of the U.S between Maine and New Brunswick.

FASCINATING FACT: Tyler was the first vice president to become president upon the death of the **incumbent**.

JOHN TYLER

VITAL STATS

Birthday: November 2, 1795
State: North Carolina
Political party: Democratic
Vice president: George M. Dallas
Age at inauguration: 49
Wife: Sarah Childress
Children: None
Date and cause of death: June 15, 1849; heart failure

HISTORICAL HAPPENINGS

★ 1846: A U.S. treaty with Great Britain added territory that later became Washington, Oregon, Idaho, and part of Montana.

★ 1846-1848: Border disputes led Congress to wage war against Mexico. As a result, the U.S. acquired California, Arizona, and New Mexico.

Baseball

The rules of baseball were standardized in 1845. The origins of the sport, however, are unclear. Abner Doubleday is often miscredited as being the "father of baseball." The sport had many contributors and can be traced to a number of English ball games, including cricket, rounders, feeder, and "this old cat."

The Speaker of the House

The party with the most members in the House of Representatives elects the Speaker of the House. As the chair of every session, no one in the House may speak until the Speaker calls on her or him. After the vice president, the Speaker is next in line for the presidency.

FASCINATING FACTS

✪ James Polk was the first "dark horse" candidate (a relatively unknown person, chosen when political party conventions become deadlocked between strong rivals) to become president.

✪ He was also the first Speaker of the House to become president.

12TH PRESIDENT OF THE UNITED STATES • TERM: 1849–1850, DIED IN OFFIC

VITAL STATS

Birthday: November 24, 1784
State: Virginia
Political party: Whig
Vice president: Millard Fillmore
Age at inauguration: 64
Wife: Margaret Mackall Smith
Children: Ann Mackall, Sarah Knox, Octavia Pannill, Margaret Smith, Mary Elizabeth, Richard
Date and cause of death: July 9, 1850; natural causes

HISTORICAL HAPPENINGS

★ 1850: Great Britain and the U.S. signed the Clayton-Bulwer Treaty, designed to guarantee the **neutrality** of a proposed canal (later the Panama Canal).

FASCINATING FACT: A religious man, Zachary Taylor refused to be **inaugurated** on a Sunday. He was inaugurated on Monday, March 5, instead. The former president, James Polk, stepped down on March 3. For one day, the president of the Senate, Senator David Rice Atchison, served as acting president.

ZACHARY TAYLOR

13TH PRESIDENT OF THE UNITED STATES • TERM: 1850–1853

VITAL STATS

Birthday: January 7, 1800
State: New York
Political party: Whig
Vice president: None
Age at inauguration: 50
Wives: Abigail Powers; Caroline Carmichael McIntosh
Children: With Abigail: Millard Powers, Mary Abigail
Date and cause of death: March 8, 1874; stroke

HISTORICAL HAPPENINGS

★ 1850: Fillmore signed the controversial Fugitive Slave Act, which required free states to return slaves to their masters. The Northern states objected and often refused to comply.

FASCINATING FACT: Oxford University offered Fillmore an honorary Doctorate of Civil Law. He turned it down, saying, "I had not the advantage of a classical education and no man should, in my judgment, accept a degree he cannot read."

MILLARD FILLMORE

14TH PRESIDENT OF THE UNITED STATES • TERM: 1853–1857

VITAL STATS

Birthday: November 23, 1804
State: New Hampshire
Political party: Democratic
Vice president: William R. King
Age at inauguration: 48

Wife: Jane Means Appleton
Children: Frank Robert, Benjamin
Date and cause of death: October 8, 1869; natural causes

HISTORICAL HAPPENINGS

★ 1854: With the help of Commodore Perry and U.S. Navy warships, the Kanagawa Treaty was signed, which opened up trade with Japan.

★ 1854: The Kansas-Nebraska Act gave settlers in the new territories the right to decide whether to allow slavery. Antislavery men in Michigan formed the **Republican party**.

FRANKLIN PIERCE

FASCINATING FACT: Franklin Pierce's nickname was Young Hickory of the Granite Hills.

15TH PRESIDENT OF THE UNITED STATES • TERM: 1857–1861

VITAL STATS

Birthday: April 23, 1791
State: Pennsylvania
Political party: Democratic
Vice president: John C. Breckinridge
Age at inauguration: 65

Wife: Unmarried
Children: None
Date and cause of death: June 1, 1868; pneumonia and heart trouble

HISTORICAL HAPPENINGS

★ 1859: Militant abolitionist John Brown led an attack on the Federal arsenal at Harper's Ferry, Virginia. His capture and execution heightened tensions that led to the Civil War.

★ 1860: The Pony Express began delivering mail between St. Joseph, Missouri, and Sacramento, California.

FASCINATING FACT: James Buchanan was the only bachelor president in U.S. history.

VITAL STATS

Birthday: February 12, 1809

State: Kentucky

Political party: Republican

Vice presidents: Hannibal Hamlin, Andrew Johnson

Age at inauguration: 52

Wife: Mary Todd

Children: Robert, Edward Baker, William Wallace, Thomas (Tad)

Date and cause of death: April 15, 1865; shot by John Wilkes Booth

"Four score and seven years ago, our fathers brought forth on this continent a new nation conceived in liberty and dedicated to the proposition that all men are created equal."
– Gettysburg Address

HISTORICAL HAPPENINGS

★ 1861: The Confederate States of America declared independence.

★ 1861-1865: The Civil War was fought between the North and the South.

★ 1863: On November 19, Lincoln gave his famous Gettysburg Address at the opening of the National Cemetery at Gettysburg, the site of a terrible Civil War battle in which five thousand men from both armies died.

President Lincoln and Union soldiers

★ 1865: On April 9, General Robert E. Lee surrendered at Appomattox. The war was over and the slaves were freed. Five days later, John Wilkes Booth, an actor who believed he was helping the South, shot and killed Lincoln while the president was watching a production of *Our American Cousin* at Ford's Theatre in Washington, D.C.

FASCINATING FACTS

✪ The Civil War began within two months of Lincoln's inauguration and ended the month he died.

✪ Eleven-year-old Grace Bedell wrote to Mr. Lincoln, advising him to grow a beard. "You would look a great deal better," she wrote, "for your face is so thin." Lincoln took her advice. He was the first president to wear a beard in office.

The Other President

When the South left the Union, Southerners elected their own president. Jefferson Davis was the first President of the Confederacy. When the Civil War ended, so did his presidency.

17TH PRESIDENT OF THE UNITED STATES • TERM: 1865–1869

VITAL STATS

Birthday: December 29, 1808
State: North Carolina
Political party: Democratic
Vice president: None
Age at inauguration: 56

Wife: Eliza McCardle
Children: Martha, Charles, Mary, Robert, Andrew Jr.
Date and cause of death: July 31, 1875; stroke

HISTORICAL HAPPENINGS

★ 1865: Congress **ratified** the Thirteenth Amendment, ending discrimination on the basis of race, religion, or creed.
★ 1865: Susan B. Anthony and other **suffragettes** began the long campaign to give women the right to vote.

FASCINATING FACTS: Johnson never went to school. His wife, Eliza, taught him to read when he was seventeen.

ANDREW JOHNSON

18TH PRESIDENT OF THE UNITED STATES • TERMS: 1869–1873, 1873–1877

VITAL STATS

Birthday: April 27, 1822
State: Ohio
Political party: Republican
Vice presidents: Schuyler Colfax, Henry Wilson
Age at inauguration: 46

Wife: Julia Boggs Dent
Children: Frederick Dent, Ulysses II, Ellen, Jess Root
Date and cause of death: July 23, 1885; throat cancer

HISTORICAL HAPPENINGS

★ 1873: Grant supported **amnesty** for Confederate leaders and **civil rights** for former slaves.
★ 1876: General George Custer and his men were massacred at the Battle of the Little Bighorn by Sioux and Cheyenne Indians.

FASCINATING FACT: When Ulysses Hiram Grant applied to West Point, he was mistakenly listed as Ulysses Simpson Grant. He never corrected the error.

ULYSSES S. GRANT

19TH PRESIDENT OF THE UNITED STATES • TERM: 1877–1881

VITAL STATS

Birthday: October 4, 1822
State: Ohio
Political party: Republican
Vice president: William A. Wheeler
Age at inauguration: 54
Wife: Lucy Ware Webb
Children: Birchard, James Webb, Rutherford Platt, Joseph Thompson, George Cook, Fanny, Scott Russell, Manning
Date and cause of death: January 17, 1893; natural causes

HISTORICAL HAPPENINGS

★ 1877: With the words, "I will fight no more forever," Chief Joseph surrendered to U.S. forces, ending the war between the U.S. government and the Nez Percé tribe.

RUTHERFORD B. HAYES

FASCINATING FACTS: Lucy Hayes was the first wife of a president to hold a college degree. She advocated women's rights and social reform. Her support of a ban on liquor earned her the nickname Lemonade Lucy.

20TH PRESIDENT OF THE UNITED STATES • TERM: 1881 (ASSASSINATED)

VITAL STATS

Birthday: November 19, 1831
State: Ohio
Political party: Republican
Vice president: Chester Alan Arthur
Age at inauguration: 49
Wife: Lucretia Rudolph
Children: Eliza Arabella, Harry Augustus, James Rudolph, Mary, Irvin McDowell, Edwin, Abram
Date and cause of death: September 19, 1881; shot by Charles Guiteau

HISTORICAL HAPPENINGS

★ 1881: Less than four months after taking office, Garfield was shot and killed by Charles Guiteau, a lawyer who wanted Chester Arthur to be president.

FASCINATING FACTS: Garfield was the first left-handed president. He was the last chief executive born in a log cabin.

JAMES A. GARFIELD

21ST PRESIDENT OF THE UNITED STATES • TERM: 1881–1885

VITAL STATS

Birthday: October 5, 1829
State: Vermont
Political party: Republican
Vice president: None
Age at inauguration: 52
Wife: Ellen Lewis Herndon
Children: William Lewis Herndon, Chester Alan, Ellen Herndon
Date and cause of death: November 18, 1886; stroke

HISTORICAL HAPPENINGS

★ 1882: Congress passes the first Chinese exclusion act, banning Chinese immigration for ten years. Both Arthur and Hayes had previously vetoed this bill.
★ 1884: Arthur's expansion of the Navy's budget allowed construction of the first steel-hulled cruisers.

FASCINATING FACT: The U.S. had three presidents in 1881: Hayes concluded his term, Garfield was elected and assassinated, and Arthur became president.

CHESTER A. ARTHU

22ND, 24TH PRESIDENT OF THE UNITED STATES • TERMS: 1885–1889, 1893–189

VITAL STATS

Birthday: March 18, 1837
State: New Jersey
Political party: Democratic
Vice presidents: Thomas Hendricks, Adlai Stevenson
Age at inauguration: 47 and 55
Wife: Frances Folson
Children: Ruth, Esther, Marion, Grover, Francis Grover
Date and cause of death: June 24, 1908; natural causes

HISTORICAL HAPPENINGS

★ 1886: The Statue of Liberty was dedicated at Liberty (formerly Bedloe's) Island in New York harbor.
★ 1894: Cleveland sent federal troops to Chicago when rioting broke out during a railroad strike.

FASCINATING FACTS: Cleveland was the only president to serve two nonconsecutive terms (before and after Harrison). The Baby Ruth candy bar was named for his daughter Ruth.

GROVER CLEVELAND

23RD PRESIDENT OF THE UNITED STATES • TERM: 1889–1893

VITAL STATS

Birthday: August 20, 1833
State: Ohio
Political party: Republican
Vice president: Levi Morton
Age at inauguration: 55
Wives: Caroline Scott, Mary Scott Lord Dimmick
Children: With Caroline: Russell Benjamin, Mary Scott
Date and cause of death: March 13, 1901; natural causes

HISTORICAL HAPPENINGS

BENJAMIN HARRISON

★ 1889: Four states were admitted to the U.S.: North Dakota, South Dakota, Montana, and Washington.
★ 1889: The first Pan-American conference paved the way for active cooperation between the U.S. and Latin America.

FASCINATING FACT: The grandson of William Henry Harrison, the ninth president of the U.S., Benjamin Harrison lost the popular vote but won the election with electoral votes.

5TH PRESIDENT OF THE UNITED STATES • TERM: 1897–1901 (ASSASSINATED)

VITAL STATS

Birthday: January 29, 1843
State: Ohio
Political party: Republican
Vice presidents: Garret A. Hobart, Theodore Roosevelt
Age at inauguration: 54
Wife: Ida Saxton
Children: Katherine, Ida
Date and cause of death: September 14, 1901; shot by Leon Czolgosz

HISTORICAL HAPPENINGS

★1897: Gold was discovered in the Yukon Territory near the Canada-Alaska border, beginning the Klondike gold rush.
★ 1898: The Spanish-American War began when the USS *Maine* was sunk in Cuba's Havana harbor.

FASCINATING FACT: McKinley was shot and killed by Leon Czolgosz, an **anarchist**, on September 6, 1901, at the Pan-American Exposition in Buffalo, New York.

THEODORE ROOSEVELT

VITAL STATS

Birthday: October 27, 1858
State: New York
Political party: Republican
Vice president: Charles Fairbanks (second term only)
Age at inauguration: 42
Wives: Alice Hathaway Lee, Edith Kermit Carow
Children: With Alice: Alice
With Edith: Theodore Jr., Quentin, Kermit, Ethel, Archibald Bullock
Date and cause of death:
January 6, 1919; heart failure

Tour the White House

When Washington was elected the first president of the new United States in 1789, there was no official residence for the top executive. The government was based in New York City, where room was made for the U.S. Congress to meet in City Hall. Washington lived in a rented house. Then, in 1790, the president and his advisers made Philadelphia the official, although temporary, capital of the United States, giving themselves ten years to prepare a permanent capital "on the river Potomac."

In 1792, many architects competed to become the designer of the new Executive Mansion. The winner was Irish-American James Hoban. The unusual way he used space—creating oval rooms, for instance—is still admired today. His design called for painting the house white and inspired the name, the White House.

Ten years may have seemed like enough time to build a house, but it wasn't. When John Adams arrived in 1800, the Executive Mansion—or Presidential Palace, as it was called then—still wasn't complete. Although he and his family moved into the six rooms that were finished, the place was a mess. Abigail Adams wrote to her daughter that it was cold and uncomfortable.

When Thomas Jefferson moved in, he had a new roof built. In 1814, during the Madison administration, the White House was burned by the British. Reconstruction was completed in 1817. Every president since then has made some change in the way the White House is decorated. Many presidents have also added sports facilities for themselves. For example, Franklin D. Roosevelt installed an indoor swimming pool, and George Bush constructed a state-of-the-art horseshoe pit.

Since the president does much of his work at home, the White House combines private living quarters for the president and his family with office space for him and his staff, meeting rooms for the Cabinet, and elegant rooms for government social affairs. Some of the rooms are open to the public; others are for the president and the First Family only.

Open these pages for an insider's look at a few of the White House's rooms.

This is the president's office, where he reads bills, talks on the phone with other world leaders, and holds meetings. The presidential seal appears all over the Oval Office: on the rug, on the ceiling, and on the front of the president's desk. Given to America's nineteenth president, Rutherford B. Hayes, by Queen Victoria of England, the desk is made of wood from the HMS *Resolute,* a nineteenth-century whaling ship.

Every president does something to personalize this room. President Clinton has photos of his family and friends on the table behind his desk. Although the president can change most

Ever since Franklin D. Roosevelt's administration, the Cabinet Room has been used for high-level meetings. A huge oval table takes up most of the room. Around this table are chairs for the president, the vice president, and the Cabinet—the president's inner circle of advisers. Each seat has a brass plaque engraved with the name of the Cabinet member who sits there. The president also uses the Cabinet Room for top-level meetings with the National Security Council.

Like all of the other rooms in the White House, the Cabinet Room holds many works of art. Marble busts of George Washington and Benjamin Franklin look out at the room from niches on either side of the fireplace. A painting that portrays the Declaration of Independence hangs above the mantel. Portraits of four presidents—Washington, Jefferson, Lincoln, and Teddy Roosevelt—are exhibited as well. When it is not being used for meetings, the Cabinet Room is used for special award ceremonies. The room overlooks the Rose Garden.

The Cabinet consists of fourteen major departments. The president appoints the head, or secretary, of each. The departments are state, treasury, interior, agriculture, justice, commerce, labor, defense, housing and urban development, transportation, energy, education, health and human services, and veterans' affairs.

The Diplomatic Reception Room, where the president greets visiting dignitaries and heads of state, was also the site of President Franklin D. Roosevelt's famous fireside chats.

Except for George Washington, every president and First Family has lived, entertained, and conducted national and international meetings in the White House.

Originally, the Lincoln Bedroom wasn't even a bedroom. It was used by many presidents—including Lincoln himself—as an office or a cabinet room. When Teddy Roosevelt was president, all of the offices in this part of the White House were moved to the West Wing. This room became part of the First Family's private quarters. It was Truman who suggested putting bedroom furniture from Lincoln's era into the room. Bought by Mrs. Lincoln, the bed is enormous—8 feet long and almost 6 feet wide. Though Honest Abe himself never slept in it, many other presidents have, including Teddy Roosevelt and Woodrow Wilson. These days, the Lincoln Bedroom is used mostly as a guest bedroom for friends of the president's family.

One of the objects in this room is definitely not from Lincoln's time: a holographic reproduction of the Gettysburg Address. This high-tech copy of one of the most famous speeches in U.S. history sits on the desk. A painting of Lincoln and his youngest son, Tad, hangs on one wall. The room also holds an engraving of an 1864 painting entitled *First Reading of the Emancipation Proclamation before Lincoln's Cabinet.* It was in this room that Lincoln rehearsed his famous proclamation abolishing slavery.

The President and First Lady host formal dinners in the State Dining Room to honor visiting royalty and foreign leaders. The State Dining Room can seat 140 people.

of the interior to suit his own tastes, two things never change position in the Oval Office—the United States flag and the presidential flag. Both flags stand behind the president's desk, the presidential flag to the chief executive's left and the U.S. flag to his right.

Like the Cabinet Room, the Oval Office holds valuable artwork. There is a "porthole portrait" (small and round like the porthole of a ship) of George Washington, and other paintings of early American life. A Frederic Remington bronze statue of a cowboy riding a bucking bronco stands near the east wall. A bronze bust of Benjamin Franklin sits on the office mantelpiece.

THE ROSE GARDEN

While gardens have been part of the White House landscape since John Adams's term in 1800, the Rose Garden didn't exist until 113 years later. Ellen Wilson, the twenty-eighth First Lady, planted the first roses outside the Cabinet Room. Her garden remained virtually unchanged for almost fifty years. In 1962, John F. Kennedy had the garden redesigned. Glass doors from the Cabinet Room open right onto the garden. The president often uses the Rose Garden to receive guests.

The Rose Garden has been the setting for many historical events. President Eisenhower received the first team of astronauts here. Sandra Day O'Connor, the first woman appointed to the Supreme Court, was received in the Rose Garden by President Reagan. During America's Bicentennial celebration, Queen Elizabeth II of Great Britain dined here. The Rose Garden was also the site of the first outdoor wedding to be held in White House history, when Tricia Nixon married Edward Cox in June, 1971.

On the South Lawn of the White House, presidents past and present have enjoyed many outdoor activities, including tennis, golf, and swimming.

TERMS: 1901–1905, 1905–1909

At the onset of the Spanish-American War, Roosevelt rounded up a band of sportsmen and Texas rangers and trained them as the first U.S. Volunteer Cavalry, known as the Rough Riders. Because of transportation problems, however, they were forced to leave their horses behind in Florida, and fought most of their battles in Cuba—including El Carey and San Juan Hill—on foot.

HISTORICAL HAPPENINGS

★ 1903: The Wright brothers (Wilbur and Orville) made the first successful powered airplane flight at Kitty Hawk, North Carolina.

★ 1905: Roosevelt helped settle the ongoing Russo-Japanese War. Roosevelt himself asked the Russian and Japanese leaders to work with an international peacemaker. Many of Roosevelt's terms for peace were included in the final treaty, which was signed aboard the president's yacht, the *Mayflower*, on September 5. For his part in negotiating the treaty, Roosevelt won the **Nobel Peace Prize** in 1906.

★ 1906: A great earthquake and fire destroyed San Francisco.

FASCINATING FACTS

✪ At his inauguration after McKinley's assassination, Roosevelt was only forty-two. He remains the youngest man ever to have taken office as president of the U.S.

✪ A lover of physical exercise, Roosevelt was a great outdoorsman. He boxed, hunted, and rode horses. During his administration, he added 125 million acres to the U.S. forest system.

✪ The statue in front of the Museum of Natural History in New York City is of Teddy Roosevelt—who hated the nickname Teddy.

✪ He was the first president to ride in a car and the first to fly in a plane.

The teddy bear was inspired by Teddy Roosevelt. On a hunting trip, the president refused to shoot a bear he had cornered because it was too small. He let it go unharmed. Teddy bears soon became wildly popular.

VITAL STATS

Birthday: September 15, 1857
State: Ohio
Political party: Republican
Vice president: James S. Sherman
Age at inauguration: 51
Wife: Helen Herron
Children: Robert, Helen, Charles Phelps
Date and cause of death: March 8, 1930; heart disease

HISTORICAL HAPPENINGS

WILLIAM H. TAFT

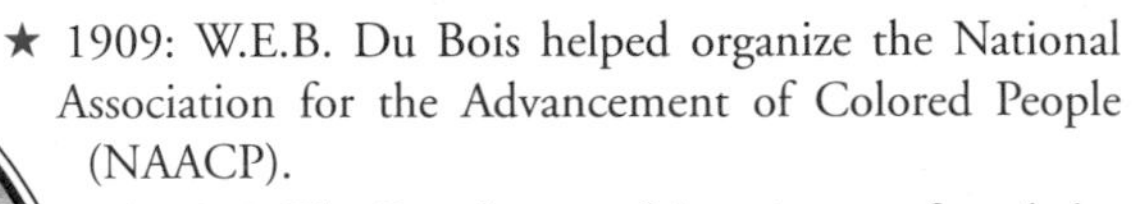

★ 1909: W.E.B. Du Bois helped organize the National Association for the Advancement of Colored People (NAACP).

★ 1910: The Boy Scouts of America was founded.

★ 1912: New Mexico and Arizona became the 47th and 48th states, respectively.

On the night of April 14, 1912, the "unsinkable" *Titanic* hit an iceberg and sank off the coast of Newfoundland. Of the 2,200 people on board, 1,500 drowned.

FASCINATING FACTS

- Taft was over six feet tall and weighed more than three hundred pounds.
- He was the first president to throw the first pitch on opening day of the baseball season, which he did on April 14, 1910, for the American League game between Washington and Philadelphia. A record-breaking crowd of 12,226 fans attended the game.
- Taft was the only man in the U.S. to serve as both president and chief justice of the Supreme Court (1921-1930).

VITAL STATS

Birthday: December 28, 1856
State: Virginia
Political party: Democratic
Vice president: Thomas Marshall
Age at inauguration: 56
Wives: Ellen Louise Axson, Edith Bolling Galt
Children: With Ellen: Margaret, Jessie, Eleanor
Date and cause of death: February 3, 1924; natural causes

HISTORICAL HAPPENINGS

WOODROW WILSON

★ 1914: World War I began in Europe.

★ 1917: German submarines sank U.S. ships. The U.S. entered World War I.

★ 1919: Congress ratified the Eighteenth Amendment, known as Prohibition. It outlawed the manufacture, sale, transportation, importation, and exportation of liquor nationwide.

★ 1920: In the aftermath of the war, the League of Nations was created. Despite Wilson's contributions, the Senate rejected the idea of U.S. membership. His efforts, however, earned him the Nobel Peace Prize in 1919.

★ 1920: Wilson appointed the first female assistant attorney general, Annette Abbott Adams.

★ 1920: Fourteen years after the death of suffragette Susan B. Anthony, the Nineteenth Amendment was passed, giving women the right to vote.

Suffragettes

FASCINATING FACTS

✪ Because of his background as a teacher and as president of Princeton University, Wilson was known as the Schoolmaster in Politics.

✪ Wilson was the first president to hold a **press conference**. He met with 125 reporters on May 15, 1913.

FROM YOUNG CHILDREN TO GROWN CHILDREN TO GRANDCHILDREN, FIRST KIDS OF ALL AGES HAVE CALLED THE WHITE HOUSE HOME.

Tad Lincoln

The youngest of Honest Abe's four sons was given the name Thomas when he was born. Tad is short for Tadpole, a nickname his father gave him because the boy's head, like a tadpole's, seemed too large for his body. Tad and his brothers liked to play army in the White House attic. Tad was also very generous. He invited homeless children to the White House for Christmas dinner.

Abraham Lincoln's youngest s Tad, pose wearing colonel's uniform.

Alice Roosevelt

Alice was the only child born to Teddy and Alice Roosevelt. Alice was seventeen when her father became president. The Roosevelt White House was famous for the number of pets the family kept. Alice had a snake named Emily Spinach. She kept the serpent in her handbag and released it on unsuspecting visitors. In 1902, Alice became the first First Daughter to have her debut in the White House. Her marriage also took place in the Executive Mansion. She and Senator Nick Longworth exchanged vows in 1906 in the East Room.

Alice and her half brothers and half sisters. From left to right: Teddy Jr., Ethel, Quentin, Kermit, and Archie

Archibald Roosevelt

Archibald Roosevelt was Alice's half brother. He was seven when his father became the 26th president of the United States. He went to Sidwell Friends Academy in 1904 when he was ten—the same school Chelsea Clinton attended later. Archie often invited his school friends home to play football on the White House lawn. Among the many Roosevelt pets was Archie's pony, Algonquin. He once brought it into the White House elevator.

John and Caroline Kennedy

John and Caroline Kennedy were two of the youngest children ever to live in the White House. Caroline was only four when her father became president. John-John was born when his father was president-elect.

John-John often came into the Oval Office and played under the desk while his father was working.

Caroline and John Jr. with their uncle, Attorney General Robert F. Kennedy, and their mother, Jacqueline, at John F. Kennedy's funeral.

Amy chats with her father, Jimmy Carter.

Amy Carter

When Amy was nine years old, she moved with her family to the White House. While she lived in Washington, D.C., Amy attended a **desegregated** public school. The Secret Service followed her everywhere, and she disliked that almost as much as she hated wearing braces on her teeth. Amy had sleepovers at the White House. She and her friends slept in Lincoln's bed and waited all night for Lincoln's ghost to show up.

Chelsea Clinton

President Clinton's daughter, Chelsea, was twelve when her father was elected. For her thirteenth birthday, February 27, 1993, Chelsea invited friends to a sleepover party at the White House. The First Teen played soccer and softball and was also a member of the drama club.

Chelsea and dad, Bill Clinton.

29TH PRESIDENT OF THE UNITED STATES • TERM: 1921–1923, DIED IN OFFIC

VITAL STATS

Birthday: November 2, 1865
State: Ohio
Political party: Republican
Vice president: Calvin Coolidge
Age at inauguration: 55
Wife: Florence Kling De Wolfe
Children: Elizabeth Ann Christian (with his mistress, Nan Britton)
Date and cause of death: August 2, 1923; stroke

HISTORICAL HAPPENINGS

★ 1921: Harding pledged a "return to normalcy" to focus on national issues following the end of World War I.

★ 1923: The Teapot Dome scandal revealed that the Secretary of the Interior had secretly leased government oil reserves to private oil companies.

WARREN G. HARDIN

FASCINATING FACT: Assessing his presidency, Harding said, "I am not fit for this office and never should have been here."

30TH PRESIDENT OF THE UNITED STATES • TERMS: 1923–1925, 1925–192

VITAL STATS

Birthday: July 4, 1872
State: Vermont
Political party: Republican
Vice president: Charles G. Dawes (second term only)
Age at inauguration: 51
Wife: Grace Anna Goodhue
Children: John, Calvin Jr.
Date and cause of death: January 5, 1933; heart disease

HISTORICAL HAPPENINGS

CALVIN COOLIDGE

★1924: Native Americans born in the U.S. were allowed to become citizens for the first time.

★ 1927: In his plane the *Spirit of St. Louis*, Charles Lindbergh became the first person to fly solo over the Atlantic Ocean. The trip from New York to Paris took 33½ hours.

FASCINATING FACT: Calvin Coolidge's first inauguration took place at his home in Plymouth, Vermont, where his father, Colonel John Calvin Coolidge, swore him in.

VITAL STATS

Birthday: August 10, 1874
State: Iowa
Political party: Republican
Vice president: Charles Curtis
Age at inauguration: 54

Wife: Lou Henry
Children: Herbert Clark Jr., Allan Henry
Date and cause of death: October 20, 1964; internal bleeding

HISTORICAL HAPPENINGS

★ 1929: On October 26, the stock market crashed, causing financial panic followed by the Great Depression. Millions of Americans lost their jobs, savings, and homes. The Depression lasted for over ten years, until the U.S. entered World War II, in 1941.

★ 1929: In Chicago, gangster Al Capone's gunmen executed seven members of the Bugs Moran gang in the St. Valentine's Day Massacre.

★ 1930: The planet Pluto was discovered by Clyde Tombaugh.

★ 1931: "The Star-Spangled Banner" became the official national anthem.

At the depth of the Depression, in 1933, one American worker in every four was out of a job. Many blamed President Hoover for the misery of millions of people. "Hoovervilles" were shantytowns built by the poor and unemployed. Newspapers were known as "Hoover blankets," and turned-out, empty pockets were "Hoover flags."

FASCINATING FACT

✪ Herbert Hoover had an asteroid named for him. Hooveria was discovered in March of 1920 by Professor Johann Palisan of the University of Vienna.

VITAL STATS

Birthday: January 30, 1882
State: New York
Political party: Democratic
Vice presidents: First and second terms: John Garner; third term: Henry Wallace; fourth term: Harry S. Truman

Age at inauguration: 51
Wife: Anna Eleanor Roosevelt
Children: Anna Eleanor, James, Elliott, Franklin Jr., John Aspinwall
Date and cause of death: April 12, 1945; cerebral hemorrhage

During the Depression, Roosevelt made many radio broadcasts to the American people. He used his famous "fireside chats" to advise and guide the public through the crisis. In his first broadcast, he urged Americans to stop hoarding cash so the banks could recover from their collapse.

HISTORICAL HAPPENINGS

★ 1933: Prohibition ended when the Twenty-first Amendment was passed. It ended the federal ban on the manufacture, sale, transportation, importation, and exportation of intoxicating beverages.

★ 1933: Roosevelt promised the country a "New Deal" to end the Great Depression, with government projects providing work for the unemployed.

★ 1941: On December 7, Japanese airplanes bombed U.S. Navy ships docked at Pearl Harbor, Hawaii. The U.S. entered World War II.

★ 1942: The first successful nuclear reaction was achieved at the University of Chicago.

FASCINATING FACTS

✪ Roosevelt contracted polio at the age of thirty-nine and was in a wheelchair during all four of his presidential terms. He rarely allowed himself to be seen in his wheelchair and insisted on standing—using crutches, a cane, or his podium—when he made public appearances. He kept his upper body strong by swimming in an indoor pool that he had installed at the White House.

✪ On April 30, 1939, he became the first media president. Roosevelt was the first president to appear on television.

✪ FDR appointed the first woman secretary of labor, Frances Perkins.

✪ FDR was elected president for four terms—and led the U.S. through two of the most critical events of its history: the Great Depression and World War II.

✪ First Lady Eleanor Roosevelt was one of America's great reforming leaders, supporting the rights of children, African Americans, women, and the poor. She was also active in the United Nations and instrumental in the drafting of the Universal Declaration of Human Rights, adopted by the UN General Assembly in 1948.

FROM COWS TO CATS, RACCOONS TO SILKWORMS, PRESIDENTS AND THEIR FAMILIES HAVE SHARED THE WHITE HOUSE WITH MANY OTHER SPECIES.

Franklin D. Roosevelt and his Scottish terrier, Fala

George Washington—Nelson, Blueskin, and other horses, ten dogs, and Martha's parrot

Thomas Jefferson—mockingbird

James Madison—Dolley's green parrot

James Monroe—dog

John Quincy Adams—alligator, silkworms

Andrew Jackson—horses

Martin Van Buren—two tiger cubs

William H. Harrison—goat, cow

John Tyler—his warhorse, the General

Zachary Taylor—his warhorse, Old Whitey

Abraham Lincoln—rabbit, ponies, dogs, turkey, pig, goats

Andrew Johnson—mice

Ulysses S. Grant—horses, parrot, dogs

Rutherford B. Hayes—cows, goats, dogs, horses, and a herd of Jersey cows. Milking the cows was supervised by Hayes's daughter, Martha.

James A. Garfield—Mary's mare, named Kit

Grover Cleveland—canaries, mockingbirds, dog

Ulysses S. Grant and one of his horses

Benjamin Harrison—goat, dogs belonging to his grandchildren

William McKinley—a parrot that sang "Yankee Doodle"

Theodore Roosevelt—horses, pony, dogs, Alice's snake named Emily Spinach, cats, badger, guinea pigs, lion, hyena, wildcat, coyote, five bears, two parrots, zebra, owl, lizards, rats, roosters, raccoon

Mildred Kerr Bush and Barbara Bush, authors of *Millie's Book*

William H. Taft—Pauline, the last White House cow

Woodrow Wilson—a tobacco-chewing ram named Old Ike, sheep

Warren G. Harding—an Airedale named Laddie Boy, a bulldog named Oh Boy, canaries

Calvin Coolidge—twelve dogs, canaries, thrush, goose, cats, raccoons, donkey, bobcat, lion cubs, pygmy hippo, bear, wallaby

Herbert Hoover—a watchdog named King Tut, and eight other dogs

Lyndon Johnson and the First Lady, known as Lady Bird, walk their beagles Him and Her

Franklin Delano Roosevelt—seven dogs

Harry S. Truman—two dogs

Dwight D. Eisenhower—a weimaraner named Heidi

John F. Kennedy—dogs, cat, canary, parakeets, Caroline's ponies Tex and Marconi, hamsters, rabbit, horse

Lyndon B. Johnson—dogs, hamsters, lovebirds

Richard M. Nixon—a cocker spaniel named Checkers

Ronald W. Reagan—dogs

George Bush—a springer spaniel named Millie

Bill Clinton—a cat named Socks

Socks, the Clintons' First Feline

VITAL STATS

Birthday: May 8, 1884
State: Missouri
Political party: Democratic
Vice president: Alben Barkley (second term only)

Age at inauguration: 60
Wife: Elizabeth Virginia Wallace
Child: Margaret
Date and cause of death: December 26, 1972; heart failure

HISTORICAL HAPPENINGS

★ 1945: Truman made the final **executive decisions** to drop atomic bombs on Hiroshima and Nagasaki, Japan, on August 6 and 9. Japan signed the formal document of surrender on September 2, ending World War II. A year later, the Atomic Energy Commission was established to control, protect, and develop atomic energy and research.

★ 1947: The Cold War, a fierce political, social, and military rivalry between the U. S. and the Soviet Union, began in the years following World War II. In this climate, Truman advanced his theory that communism would spread if not stopped. In the mid-1950s, Senator Joseph McCarthy created panic among government officials and others through his sensational and unproved accusations of Communist **subversion**.

★ 1947: The Marshall Plan gave financial support to countries devastated by World War II.

★ 1950: North Korea launched an attack on South Korea. U.S. and UN forces were sent to aid South Korea.

The bombs dropped on Hiroshima and Nagasaki killed over 100,000 people. Thousands more died from burns and radiation.

FASCINATING FACTS

✪ President Truman's middle initial *S* is not short for anything. The letter *S* is his middle name.

✪ The press was so sure that Truman would lose the 1948 election, it printed newspapers proclaiming his defeat.

VITAL STATS

Birthday: October 14, 1890
State: Texas
Political party: Republican
Vice president: Richard M. Nixon (both terms)
Age at inauguration: 62
Wife: Mamie Geneva Doud
Children: Dwight Doud, John Sheldon Doud
Date and cause of death:
March 28, 1969; heart failure

HISTORICAL HAPPENINGS

DWIGHT D. EISENHOWER

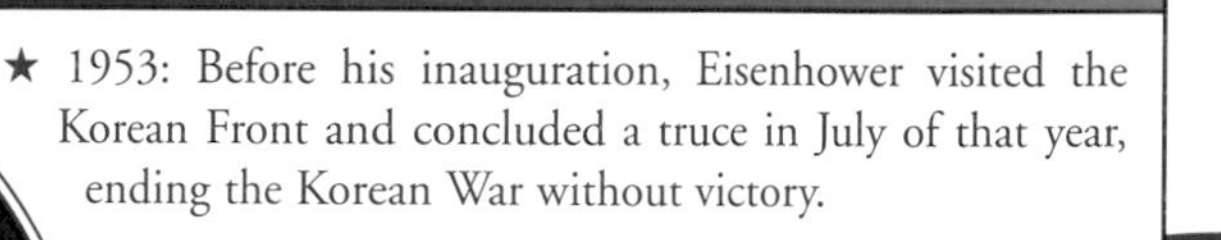

★ 1953: Before his inauguration, Eisenhower visited the Korean Front and concluded a truce in July of that year, ending the Korean War without victory.

★ 1954: The Supreme Court ordered desegregation of schools so that blacks and whites could go to school together. Three years later, Eisenhower sent troops to Little Rock, Arkansas, to protect the first black children in the city to go to a white school.

★ 1957: The Soviet Union launched the satellite *Sputnik*, and with it the race for space began.

★ 1959: Alaska and Hawaii became the 49th and 50th states, respectively.

★ 1960: In his famous "military-industrial complex" speech, Eisenhower warned of the massive potential for "misplaced power" that large military expenditures involve.

FASCINATING FACTS

✪ Eisenhower was the Supreme Allied Commander in World War II and responsible for the successful invasion of Europe. He led more than three million men on **D-Day**, June 6, 1944. When he took office, he joined a long line of generals—including Washington, Jackson, and Taylor—who became president.

✪ Eisenhower was the first president to appear on color TV, on NBC's "Home Show," on June 7, 1955.

✪ In 1958, Eisenhower signed a bill that created the National Aeronautics and Space Administration (NASA).

VITAL STATS

Birthday: May 29, 1917
State: Massachusetts
Political party: Democratic
Vice president: Lyndon B. Johnson
Age at inauguration: 43

Wife: Jacqueline Lee Bouvier
Children: Caroline, Patrick, John Fitzgerald Jr.
Date and cause of death: November 22, 1963; shot by Lee Harvey Oswald

HISTORICAL HAPPENINGS

JOHN F. KENNEDY

★ 1961: The **Peace Corps** was established.

★ 1961: Russian cosmonaut Yuri Gagarin became the first man to orbit Earth. U.S. astronauts Alan Shepard and Gus Grissom were sent into space that same year. In 1962, John Glenn Jr. became the first U.S. astronaut to orbit Earth.

★ 1962: Federal troops were sent to the University of Mississippi to protect black students who were attending the formerly all-white school.

★ 1963: The Nuclear Test Ban Treaty with Great Britain and Russia was signed.

★ 1963: Civil rights leader Martin Luther King Jr. led 250,000 blacks and whites in the March on Washington for civil rights. There, on the steps of the Lincoln Memorial, he delivered his famous "I Have a Dream" speech.

"Now is the time to open the doors of opportunity to all of God's children. Now is the time to lift our nation from the quicksands of racial injustice to the solid rock of brotherhood."
—"I Have a Dream," Martin Luther King Jr.

FASCINATING FACTS

✪ Kennedy was the first U.S. president born in the twentieth century.

✪ People are still debating JFK's assassination: Was it a conspiracy, or was just one man, Lee Harvey Oswald, responsible?

VITAL STATS

Birthday: August 27, 1908
State: Texas
Political party: Democratic
Vice president: Hubert Humphrey (second term only)

Age at inauguration: 55
Wife: Claudia Alta Taylor
Children: Lynda Byrd, Luci Baines
Date and cause of death: January 22, 1973; heart attack

HISTORICAL HAPPENINGS

★ 1964: U.S. involvement in the Vietnam War intensified when LBJ approved the bombing of North Vietnam. The Gulf of Tonkin Resolution, which allowed the president to act as he felt necessary to protect U.S. forces or South Vietnam, was passed. It allowed LBJ to **escalate** the fighting in Vietnam into a full-scale war, a war that Congress never declared.

★ 1964-1965: Johnson moved to fight a "War on Poverty" and to build a "Great Society." To that end, he pushed through Congress the Civil Rights Act, the Voting Rights Act, Medicare, and aid to education.

★ 1966: The National Organization for Women was founded to promote full equality between men and women in all walks of life.

Robert F. Kennedy

★ 1967: The first African American justice, Thurgood Marshall, was appointed to the Supreme Court.

★ 1968: Martin Luther King Jr. was shot and killed in Memphis, Tennessee.

★ 1968: Having just won the California **primary** in his own bid for the presidency, Robert F. Kennedy, brother of JFK, was assassinated.

FASCINATING FACTS

✪ When she was a little girl, Claudia Alta Taylor was nicknamed Lady Bird.

✪ All four members of the Johnson family had the initials *LBJ*.

VITAL STATS

Birthday: January 9, 1913
State: California
Political party: Republican
Vice presidents: Spiro Agnew, Gerald Ford

Age at inauguration: 56
Wife: Thelma Patricia Ryan
Children: Tricia, Julie
Date and cause of death: April 22, 1994; stroke

HISTORICAL HAPPENINGS

★ 1969: On July 20, Neil Armstrong became the first person to walk on the moon. On August 15, 500,000 young people gathered on a 600-acre farm for a two-day rock and folk music festival called Woodstock.

★ 1970: The National Guard was sent to Kent State University to control demonstrators protesting the Vietnam War. The troops opened fire and killed four students.

★ 1972: In his historic visit to Beijing, China, Nixon reversed U.S. foreign policy by recognizing the Communist government of China and opening lines of communication.

★ 1973: The Paris Accords, signed on January 31, "ended" the Vietnam War. U.S. troops withdrew a few months later.

★ 1973: The military draft was ended.

★ 1974: The Watergate hearings, which investigated the coverup of the 1972 burglary of Democratic party headquarters, established that Nixon and his staff had attempted to obstruct justice and abuse power. Rather than face **impeachment**, Nixon resigned on August 9.

First man on the moon, 1969

FASCINATING FACTS

✪ Nixon was the first president in history to resign. He was pardoned by President Gerald Ford on September 8, 1974.

38TH PRESIDENT OF THE UNITED STATES • TERM: 1974–1977

VITAL STATS

Birthday: July 14, 1913
State: Nebraska
Political party: Republican
Vice president: Nelson Rockefeller
Age at inauguration: 61
Wife: Elizabeth Bloomer
Children: Michael Gerald, John Gardner, Steven Meigs, Susan Elizabeth

GERALD R. FORD

HISTORICAL HAPPENINGS

★ 1975: The U.S.-supported regime in Vietnam was overthrown by the Communists and Vietnam was united under Communist rule soon after. The last Americans in Saigon were airlifted from the roof of the U.S. embassy.

★ 1975: On July 18, the first U.S./U.S.S.R. space linkup was made when the *Apollo* spacecraft and the *Soyuz* spacecraft met in orbit.

FASCINATING FACT: Ford survived two assassination attempts. On September 5, 1975, Lynette (Squeaky) Fromme tried to shoot him; seventeen days later, another woman tried.

39TH PRESIDENT OF THE UNITED STATES • TERM: 1977–1981

VITAL STATS

Birthday: October 1, 1924
State: Georgia
Political party: Democratic
Vice president: Walter Mondale
Age at inauguration: 52
Wife: Rosalynn Smith
Children: John William, James Earl III (Chip), Donnel Jeffrey, Amy Lynn

HISTORICAL HAPPENINGS

★ 1979: On March 26, Carter's negotiations brought about the signing of the Camp David accords between Egypt and Israel.

★ 1979: Trade was established with Communist China. On March 28, the Three Mile Island nuclear plant suffered a radiation leak.

★ 1980: Protesting the Soviet invasion of Afghanistan, the U.S. boycotted the 1980 Summer Olympics in Moscow.

FASCINATING FACTS: James Earl Carter Jr. was the first U.S. president sworn into office using a nickname. Jimmy Carter was the first president from the South in over one hundred years.

40TH PRESIDENT OF THE UNITED STATES • TERMS: 1981–1985, 1985–198

VITAL STATS

Birthday: February 6, 1911
State: Illinois
Political party: Republican
Vice president: George Bush
Age at inauguration: 69

Wives: Jane Wyman, Nancy Davis
Children: with Jane: Maureen, Michael Edward; with Nancy: Patricia Ann, Ronald Prescott

HISTORICAL HAPPENINGS

RONALD W. REAGA

★ 1981: Reagan appointed the first female Supreme Court justice, Sandra Day O'Connor.

★ 1986: The Iran-contra scandal revealed that members of Reagan's staff secretly sold weapons to Iran and used the profits to support a civil war in Nicaragua.

★ 1988: With Soviet Union leader Mikhail Gorbachev, Reagan signed a treaty to eliminate medium-range nuclear missiles.

FASCINATING FACT: Reagan was the only professional actor to become president.

41ST PRESIDENT OF THE UNITED STATES • TERM: 1989–1993

VITAL STATS

Birthday: June 12, 1924
State: Massachusetts
Political party: Republican
Vice president: Dan Quayle

Age at inauguration: 64
Wife: Barbara Pierce
Children: George, Robin, John, Neil, Marvin, Dorothy

HISTORICAL HAPPENINGS

★ 1989: The **Berlin Wall** came down, reuniting East and West Germany after 45 years. Communism began to fail throughout Eastern Europe, eventually leading to the breakup of the Soviet Union.

★ 1991: Following congressional approval, Bush ordered U.S.-led international forces to drive Iraqi invaders from oil-rich Kuwait.

FASCINATING FACT: Bush had a special all-weather horseshoe pit installed at the White House so that he could play his favorite game.

VITAL STATS

Birthday: August 19, 1946
State: Arkansas
Political party: Democratic
Vice president: Albert Gore
Age at inauguration: 46
Wife: Hillary Rodham
Child: Chelsea

HISTORICAL HAPPENINGS

BILL CLINTON

★ 1992: Clinton signed the North American Free Trade Agreement (NAFTA), encouraging trade between Mexico, Canada, and the U.S.

★ 1992: After the 1992 congressional elections, Republicans held a majority of seats in Congress for the first time in twelve years.

★ 1994: On February 3, Clinton made the highly controversial decision to lift the U.S. embargo on trade with Vietnam.

★ 1995: Clinton sent U.S. troops to join an international peacekeeping mission to help put an end to the civil war in the former Yugoslavia.

★ 1996: Congress approved a Welfare Reform Bill that would cut back welfare payments.

FASCINATING FACTS

✪ Bill Clinton was originally named William Blythe. His name was changed several years after he was adopted by his mother's second husband, Roger Clinton.

✪ During his campaign in 1992, Clinton played the saxophone on late-night television. The performance increased his popularity and recognition among young voters nationwide.

"I do solemnly swear (or affirm) that

I will faithfully execute the office of

President of the United States

and will to the best of my ability,

preserve, protect, and defend the

Constitution of the United States."

Abolitionist — A person who supports the abolition—or ending—of slavery.

Amendment — An addition to the Constitution of the United States.

Amnesty — When the government agrees not to prosecute a group or individual that has broken the law, usually during a war or crisis.

Anarchist — One who rebels against any authority, established order, or ruling power.

Assassinate — To kill by sudden or secret attack.

Berlin Wall — A wall built of concrete blocks and barbed wire, built in 1961 to keep people from fleeing from East to West Germany.

Bill — Before a new law can be passed, it must be written as a bill. Then the bill must be approved by the House of Representatives, then the Senate, and finally the president.

Checks and Balances — A system that prevents any single individual or branch of government from gaining absolute power.

Civil Rights — The individual rights of a citizen, especially the rights of personal liberty guaranteed to all Americans by the Constitution.

Congress — The House of Representatives and the Senate combined. The word *congress* means "union."

Constitution — The basic principles and laws of the U.S. that determine the powers and duties of the government and guarantee certain rights to the people, in effect since 1789.

D-Day — June 6, 1944, when Allied forces began the invasion of France in World War II.

Democracy — A government that is run by elected officials. The people elect leaders to make and enforce laws and conduct business for the common good.

Democratic Party — One of the oldest American political parties. It was formed before the Republican party.

Democratic-Republican Party — Formed by Thomas Jefferson, this political party wanted to give more power to individual citizens and states than to the national government.

Desegregated — No longer racially separated. A desegregated school is one that students of all races attend.

Embargo — An order by a government prohibiting the departure of commercial ships from its ports.

Escalate — To increase in extent, number, or amount.

Executive Decision — A decision made by the president that does not need the approval of Congress.

Federalist Party — Federalists believed in a powerful central government.

Founding Father — A member of the American Constitutional Convention of 1787.

House of Representatives — The house of Congress made up of representatives from each state. A number of representatives—based on the population of each state—are elected every two years.

Impeachment — The removal of a president or other government official from office after they are convicted of a crime.

Inaugurate — To usher into office with a formal ceremony.

Incumbent — A person who holds an office.

Neutrality — Refusal to take part in a war between other powers.

Nobel Peace Prize — Alfred Nobel was the inventor of dynamite. When he died in 1896, his will established cash prizes to be given annually to those who work for the betterment of humanity. Nobel prizes are awarded for achievements in six categories: physics, chemistry, medicine, literature, economics, and world peace.

Peace Corps — A U.S. government agency that trains and sends volunteers to assist developing nations.